Everything You Need to Know About

Smoking

Teenage smoking in the United States could claim millions of lives in the future.

Everything You Need to Know About **Smoking**

Elizabeth Keyishian

Series Editor: Evan Stark, Ph.D.

The Rosen Publishing Group, Inc.
New York

Published in 1989, 1993, 1995, 1997, 2000, 2003 by The Rosen Publishing
Group, Inc.
29 East 21st Street, New York, NY 10010

Library of Congress Cataloging-in-Publication Data

Keyishian, Elizabeth
Everything you need to know about smoking / by Elizabeth Keyishian
   p. cm. — (The need to know library)
Includes bibliographical references and index.
ISBN 0-8239-4092-6
1. Tobacco habit—Juvenile literature. 2. Smoking—Juvenile literature.
3. Youth—Tobacco use—Juvenile literature. [1. Smoking.] I. Title. II. Title:
Smoking. III. Series.
HV5745.K48 1989
813.85—dc20

                        89-10256

Manufactured in the United States of America

Contents

Introduction

Have you heard someone say that he or she is trying to quit smoking? This person has a tough challenge ahead. Fortunately, the person is not alone, and there are several ways to get help. According to the National Institutes of Health (NIH), more than 35 million people try to quit smoking each year. The Centers for Disease Control and Prevention (CDC) estimates that this is about 70 percent of all smokers. Teens—and even preteens—are a part of this group. According to the American Lung Association (ALA), in 2000, more than 50 percent of middle school and high school smokers also tried to quit.

Smoking is a habit that is not easy to break. Many smokers wish that they had never started smoking.

Perhaps they started because "everyone was doing it" or because they thought it would make them seem cool or more grown up. Perhaps they didn't know any better.

Cigarettes are addictive because they contain nicotine. Nicotine is a powerful and addictive drug. It is also a poison. A large amount of nicotine injected directly into the bloodstream could kill a human in less than an hour. Nicotine is what gives you a "buzz," or a high, when you smoke. It hooks you and keeps you coming back for more. Even if someone successfully quits, it is not uncommon for him or her to start smoking again as much as a year or more after the last cigarette.

According to the ALA, there are about 4.5 million teen smokers right now. Each day, about 4,800 young people between the ages of eleven and seventeen try their first cigarette. Almost 2,000 of these teens will become daily smokers. If you ask these teens if they think they will still be smoking in five years, 75 percent of them will say no. They are wrong. According to a study by the CDC, only 13.5 percent successfully stop. Most teen smokers report that they would love to quit but are unable to do so.

Many people, especially teens, want to be cool, to fit in, and to have friends. However, picking up a harmful, potentially lifelong habit does not make a

Many teenagers think of smoking as a social activity that helps them relax, but they don't consider the high risks of illness and death associated with smoking.

person cool. What also isn't cool is that smoking causes death. From 1995 to 1999, the ALA found that smoking killed more than 440,000 Americans each year. It kills about 40,000 Canadians each year. According to the Canadian Lung Association, each smoked cigarette will take at least five minutes off of a person's life. After ten cigarettes, a smoker has already made his or her life shorter by fifty minutes. Think about it: Smoking is not healthy because it causes illness. Smoking-related illnesses include the following.

- ◎ Lung cancer and other smoking-related cancers

- ◎ Heart disease

- ◎ Stained teeth and bad breath

- ◎ Respiratory problems such as coughing and wheezing

- ◎ Loss of the ability to smell and taste

- ◎ Infertility problems in women

Smoking addiction also means big business for tobacco companies. The entire tobacco industry is a multibillion dollar business. Each year, more than one million smokers successfully quit. Tobacco companies use advertising to attract new smokers. They target young adults, especially teens, because they are just starting to make choices about their lives. Clever yet deceptive advertising makes smoking seem like a lifestyle choice that is fun, rewarding, and socially acceptable. According to the ALA, the tobacco industry spent more than $8.2 billion on advertising in 1999. That is a lot of money being spent to get you interested in a deadly habit.

Cigarette advertisements do not tell the whole story. Tobacco companies are now paying a price for not revealing the health risks associated with smoking.

Across the country, they are being sued for millions of dollars by smokers with smoking-related health problems and by the families of people who have died from smoking-related illnesses. Many cases are settled out of court. This means that tobacco companies give money to the smokers and smokers' families so that the cases do not go to court. This prevents tobacco companies from getting bad publicity. It also keeps all the facts about smoking and related health problems from being easily known.

Now that you have learned some of the facts, do you still think smoking sounds cool? Is smoking really worth the damage that it will cause your body? Deciding whether to smoke is your choice. While making that choice, be aware of the risks involved. This book will help you understand your options, give you some important facts to think about, and prepare you to make a decision that, in the end, could be a matter of life and death.

Chapter 1

The Health Risks of Smoking

Why do people start smoking? Many young people start smoking because other people around them do. Their parents, brothers and sisters, relatives, or friends smoke, so it does not seem like a big deal. You may even think that you should smoke because others do and you want to be like them. Fortunately, we can admire someone without picking up his or her bad habits. You can still admire the smokers in your life, even while knowing that smoking is a dead end.

The media sometimes shows us that smoking is a sign of freedom, rebellion, or being fashionable. An action hero in a movie may light up a cigarette after getting the bad guys. A high-powered and stressed-out financial wiz may take a long drag on a cigarette during a deal.

Smoking does not appear to be dangerous because so many people seem to be doing it, and there do not seem to be any negative side effects. Fortunately, many states have restrictions about cigarette promotion and use in the media. Also, the theatrical industry has made attempts to limit the use of cigarettes as props in recent years.

Even though smoking may be presented as a casual choice, it is really a big deal. The nicotine in cigarettes has been found to be more addictive than crack cocaine or alcohol. The younger you are when you start, the harder it is to quit as an adult. In other words, you may think that you can smoke a cigarette here and there in social situations, and that's it. It is not that simple, however.

Without even knowing it, you can become addicted to smoking just by having an occasional cigarette. After smoking a few cigarettes, your body starts to crave nicotine. In one study, 90 percent of young people who tried to stop smoking experienced withdrawal symptoms. Withdrawal symptoms are signs that the body still craves something. In this case, it's nicotine. These are some withdrawal symptoms of smoking.

- ◎ **Dry mouth**
- ◎ **Sore throat, gums, or tongue**
- ◎ **Coughing**
- ◎ **Headaches**

- ◎ Sleeping troubles
- ◎ Irregularity (not going to the bathroom on a regular basis)
- ◎ Fatigue
- ◎ Hunger
- ◎ Tenseness, irritability

Remember, smoking is not something that you have to do. If you never do it, you will never miss it, and you will never experience the struggle of addiction. Smoking is not something that you would naturally do, like eating or sleeping. So why even start?

Still, it might be hard if you have friends who start smoking and want you to try it, too. You may feel pressure to light up with your friends so that you can fit in and be part of the group. The main thing to remember, though, is that your body is yours and no one else's. You will suffer the consequences of what smoking does to your body, and you will also be hurting people around you with the secondhand smoke of cigarettes. Secondhand smoke is the smoke that fills the air from a lit cigarette and a smoker's lungs. It is your choice whether to smoke, but know that smoking is not an easy habit to end. You will find that standing up to peer pressure is much easier than standing up to nicotine dependence.

It can get confusing when you see adults smoke. You may wonder why someone grown up would make a choice like smoking if it is wrong. You may even start smoking so that you feel like an adult. Chances are, if you asked any adult smokers, they'd tell you not to do it. These adults are using a substance that has a powerful addiction cycle. Besides, it doesn't make you seem older, but it does age your skin. This means wrinkles and saggy skin. If you want to feel like a grown-up, make good choices about your health.

You can tell that smoking is bad for you by the way your body reacts to it. The first time you smoke, it usually makes you cough. You may choke or feel dizzy. You may even feel sick enough to throw up. Cigarette smoke contains tar, which stays in your lungs even though you blow the smoke back out through your nose or mouth. Tar in your lungs can cause cancer. Smoking can also cause heart disease and other serious health problems. Even if you do enjoy smoking, is the pleasure worth sacrificing your health or even your life?

The Health Risks

We have learned that smoking can lead to heart disease and lung cancer. The NIH found that 90 percent of all lung cancer cases are linked to smoking. Recently, however, a study reported that there is a link between cigarette smoking and colon cancer. If you start smoking when you are young, the increased risk of colon

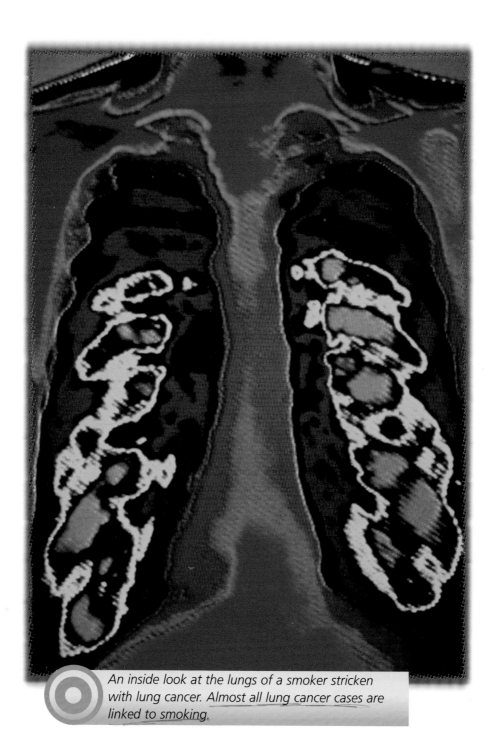

An inside look at the lungs of a smoker stricken with lung cancer. Almost all lung cancer cases are linked to smoking.

cancer stays with you even after you quit. In other words, smoking can cause permanent damage. Other cancers associated with smoking are the following.

- ◉ Mouth
- ◉ Pharynx
- ◉ Larynx
- ◉ Esophagus
- ◉ Stomach
- ◉ Pancreas
- ◉ Cervix
- ◉ Kidney
- ◉ Bladder

It may not seem important now, but your body and its health are important. Your body must be able to last through your young and middle years to a healthy old age. Many adults try to improve the health of their bodies so that they can live longer. You may probably become one of these adults, so why not get a head start? Why not try to avoid certain diseases that are linked to smoking?

Icky Ingredients

To understand how terrible smoking is for you, look at what each cigarette contains.

◎ Nicotine, a habit-forming drug

◎ Black tars that stick to the lining of your lungs and make it hard to breathe

◎ Chemicals that are poisonous and that poison your body. These chemicals include arsenic, carbon monoxide, nitrogen oxide, cyanide, and ammonia

◎ DDT, which is an insecticide (a poison for killing insects)

Every drag on a cigarette leaves those things in your lungs. In addition, nicotine speeds up your heart and makes you feel shaky. You quickly become addicted to it.

Tars coats the inside of your lungs and makes it hard to breathe. Your heart has to work harder. It is not getting enough oxygen from your stuffed-up lungs. Carbon monoxide prevents oxygen from reaching your heart. That can cause heart disease.

Your body is like a sensitive machine. The various parts of the body work together to keep you healthy. When you smoke, you damage many parts of the machine, which makes it break down. Soon the machine stops working.

According to the ALA, each of us breathes about 3,400 gallons of air each day. You breathe all day long. You take

This picture depicts the damaged tissue of a smoker's lung. Most of the time, you may not notice how smoking damages your body.

about 600 million breaths during your lifetime. It's easy to take breathing for granted. When was the last time you noticed that you were breathing? You probably have too many other things to think about. You think about breathing only when it hurts or becomes hard to breathe. Smoking will change breathing from a natural, unnoticeable activity to a difficult experience.

Try running up a flight of stairs. Your breathing increases to allow your lungs to take in more oxygen. Your heart rate increases. Your body naturally and easily adjusts to the increased demands on it (the increased demand is running). A smoker does not have it so easy.

The ingredients from smoking that are left behind in the body make natural activities harder. It is harder for the body to adjust to increased demands. There are pictures that can show you what happens to your lungs and heart when you smoke. Surgeons who operate on smokers say that the lungs are black from tar instead of the normal, healthy pink.

The lungs bring oxygen into the body and pump carbon dioxide out. Two tubes called bronchi lead to the lungs. Branches of the tubes lead into tiny balloon-like sacs. Tiny hairs brush mucus out of the airways. These hairs are called cilia.

Nicotine, the drug in tobacco, paralyzes your cilia. According to the Canadian Lung Association, even one cigarette can slow down the cilia, preventing them from working properly. Large amounts of smoke kill the cilia. The cilia cannot push the mucus out of the way, so your airways get clogged. Tars and chemicals settle in the airways, and the cilia die. The smoker has to cough to get the mucus out of the lungs. That is known as smoker's cough. It sounds as if the person is choking and wheezing. The bronchi get sore with all that coughing. The smoker then develops chronic bronchitis. It becomes more painful and difficult to breathe.

People with bronchitis often develop emphysema. This is a disease that makes it hard to breathe. Many of these people have to use a wheelchair. Simple movements, like walking and breathing, become hard to perform. You may have seen someone with emphysema. People with emphysema often take a cart carrying a heavy tank of oxygen wherever they go. Just think, the people who developed emphysema from smoking went from carrying around one little cigarette to carrying around a device that helps them breathe. That's a big change, and it all starts with one choice to start smoking.

People who smoke for a long time may also get cancer. Chemicals from smoking affect the cells of the body. They can cause the cells to grow abnormally or out of control. The cells form lumps, or tumors. Not all tumors are cancerous. Smoking does, however, cause cells to become cancerous. The tumors that form because of smoking are cancerous. These tumors block breathing. The cancer may even spread to other parts of the body.

Fortunately, your body may be able to fight the effects of smoking once you have stopped. The body begins to repair itself. The body begins to rebuild damaged cells. It slowly cleanses the lungs that are black and damaged from smoking. Eventually, the body may return to a healthy state.

Special Health Risks for Women

Smoking is dangerous for everybody, but there are special health risks for women. More and more females,

Smoking increases the risk of lung cancer, heart attack, and severe birth defects in children whose mothers smoke while pregnant.

ages fourteen to seventeen, are smoking in spite of these health risks. That might be due to cigarette advertising. It may also be because they think that cigarettes help keep their weight down. This is not true, however.

Smoking may make people feel less hungry. Many smokers believe that it provides something to do besides snack. While you may be keeping your hands and mouth busy with smoking, you're damaging your body. A person thinks that he or she is losing weight, but what's really happening is his or her health is being ruined. There are many other ways to lower or maintain your weight. You can still eat snacks, just pick something healthy, such as fruit. Sports and exercise

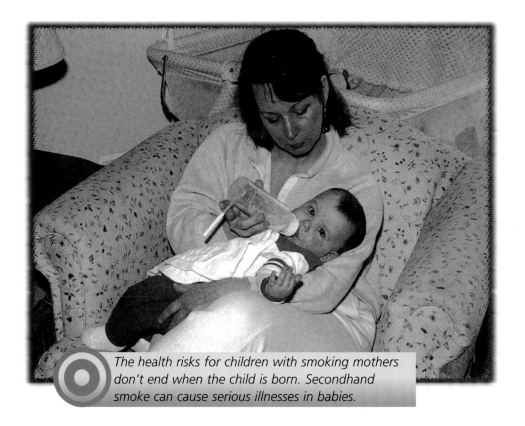

The health risks for children with smoking mothers don't end when the child is born. Secondhand smoke can cause serious illnesses in babies.

are fun ways to spend time with friends, and these activities keep your body strong and healthy. They are also other ways to maintain your weight.

Lung cancer has replaced breast cancer as the leading killer disease of women, though more women are diagnosed with breast cancer than with lung cancer. If you smoke and take birth control pills, you are ten times more likely to have a heart attack or stroke. As you age, especially over thirty-five, these risks increase. Smoking increases the risk of heart attack for young women more than any other factor. You do not have to be old to have a heart attack.

Remember the warning label on cigarette packaging: "Smoking by pregnant women may result in fetal injury, premature birth, and low birth weight." Why should you worry about that now? It may not seem important to you yet, but once you start smoking, it is very, very hard to quit. When you become a mother, you may still be smoking.

Babies of mothers who smoke have twice the risk of sudden infant death syndrome (SIDS). This disease kills babies suddenly in their sleep. Also, the babies of smokers have twice as many lung illnesses, such as bronchitis and pneumonia.

Chapter 2

What You See Is Not What You Get

Cigarette advertisers have a hard task to do. They must create ads that make smoking seem like a great thing. Smoking has to look good enough for you to want to try it, even though the ad, by law, has to warn you that smoking is harmful. This law was passed so that everyone would know the dangers of smoking.

Older people who smoke do not need advertising to convince them. A lot of people who smoke would stop if they could, but they are hooked. Smoking is a habit. Many people become addicted to the nicotine in tobacco. Their bodies need it, and they feel sick or nervous if they do not smoke.

Most adults who don't smoke will not be swayed into smoking by cigarette ads. At their age, they probably already know the truth. This is why tobacco companies target younger audiences. They want to reach the easy sale, or the customer who doesn't yet know the dangers of smoking. They want to reach young people who are beginning to define themselves. Young people experiment and search for different ways of expressing themselves. Cigarette advertisers want to tell you that you'll be cool if you smoke.

Cigarette ads make it look as if you will have fun because you smoke. They make you think that smoking will make you popular. That kind of advertising suggestion is called association. Association means linking one idea with another. Cigarette ads try to link pleasant things with their product.

Often the ads show people outdoors playing sports. In real life, people who smoke a lot can have trouble breathing. Smoking makes it hard to play active sports. If you are on a team, the coach will tell you not to smoke.

Cigarette ads show people who are healthy, with glowing skin and brilliant white teeth. In truth, smoking stains your teeth. It makes your skin dull, and it makes your hair smell bad.

Although it is against the law to sell cigarettes to minors (people younger than eighteen), cigarette ads seem to be directed toward younger and younger kids.

Congressman Henry Waxman addresses reporters in January 1998 about his efforts to combat the tobacco industry's attempts to target younger smokers.

According to a recent study conducted by the ALA, more than 30 percent of teens began smoking because of a tobacco company's advertising activities. Fortunately, there are government agencies and private organizations that are fighting to protect you from this kind of advertising trick. In 1996, the Food and Drug Administration issued regulations to limit the advertising of cigarettes and smoking to young people. These regulations include a ban on tobacco billboards within one thousand feet of schools and playgrounds. Cigarette vending machines are also not allowed anywhere that children are expected to be. Many people think that cigarette advertising should not be allowed. It is no longer allowed on television. In New York City, cigarette advertising is no longer allowed on buses or subways.

Some companies have even used cartoon characters to advertise cigarettes. The R. J. Reynolds Tobacco Company recently retired their cartoon character, Joe Camel. A 1991 study by J. R. DiFranza, J. W. Richards, and other associates showed that children responded to Joe Camel. The study showed that children as young as three years old knew who Joe Camel was and that he was associated with cigarettes. In November 1998, the outcome of a multistate settlement with the tobacco industry banned the use of cartoon characters for tobacco advertising. This means that the tobacco industry agreed to stop using characters like Joe Camel to sell its products.

Cigarette makers would never publicly reveal the hazards of cigarette smoking, or they would lose huge amounts of money. Recently they have been sued in several states for not being truthful about the health risks. In March 1999, a jury in Oregon ordered the tobacco company Philip Morris to pay $81 million to the family of a man who smoked Marlboro cigarettes for forty years before he died. In July 1999, a Florida jury ruled that cigarettes caused lung cancer and other diseases and that the makers intended to keep the dangers hidden from the public. Lawsuits against tobacco companies are increasing across the country.

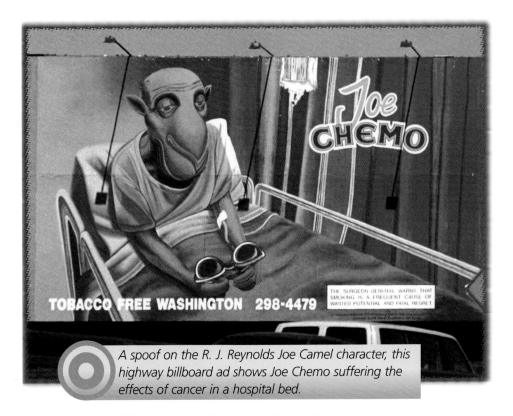

A spoof on the R. J. Reynolds Joe Camel character, this highway billboard ad shows Joe Chemo suffering the effects of cancer in a hospital bed.

A Different Kind of Advertising

There is another side to more recent cigarette advertising. Health-related groups like the American Cancer Society and the American Heart Association have ads, too. Their ads warn of the dangers of smoking.

Getting out the message about the dangers of smoking is very important. The cigarette companies spend more than $8 billion a year to convince people that smoking is not bad for them. Now there is something being done to let people know the truth about smoking.

Chapter 3

Smoking: A Hard Habit to Break

Every day we hear about the horrors of drug addiction. We read in the news about people overdosing on heroin or killing somebody to get money for crack. These are extreme cases of addiction, and most of us wouldn't guess that cigarettes are in the same category.

Like alcohol, nicotine is a legal drug. That does not make it any less of a drug, however. It may not have the immediate drastic effects of heroin or crack, but like those drugs, it is addictive. Smokers crave nicotine. They continue to smoke even though they know that it is harming them. Smokers often go through withdrawal and relapse after quitting. These things characterize drug addiction.

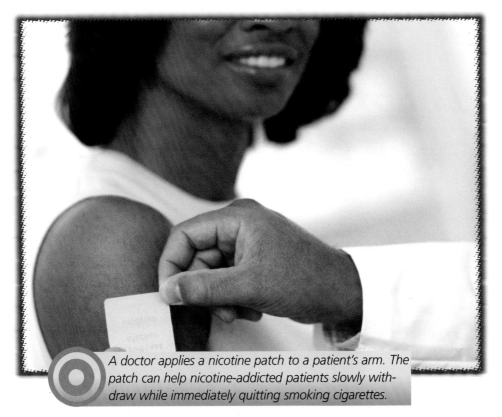

A doctor applies a nicotine patch to a patient's arm. The patch can help nicotine-addicted patients slowly withdraw while immediately quitting smoking cigarettes.

When Nicotine Takes Over

Nicotine levels range from high to low in a person's bloodstream. A low nicotine level means that there isn't a great deal of nicotine circulating through the bloodstream. When the nicotine level in the bloodstream gets low, the body signals the mind: "Smoke a cigarette. I need nicotine." As soon as the smoker lights up, the nicotine is drawn into the lungs. From the lungs, it is quickly absorbed into the bloodstream. The body's nicotine craving is satisfied, for a while.

Nicotine is a sneaky drug. When you first start smoking, you will find that it gives you a little burst of energy. That is the nicotine speeding up your heart. After a while, you will notice that you feel tired between cigarettes. That happens when the nicotine level gets low. The tired feeling is your body's way of telling you that it wants nicotine.

The smoker is stuck in a drug cycle. It's as if he or she is stuck on a seesaw. When you are "down" on the seesaw, your body feels withdrawal. That is what makes you feel tired and sluggish. Your body wants its dose of nicotine.

As you smoke a cigarette, you go "up" on the seesaw. Nicotine speeds up the heart, and it gives you a rush. It stimulates the adrenal gland. That is the gland that makes adrenaline. Adrenaline is the stuff that pumps through your veins when you are excited or nervous. Nicotine gives you a rush, but when its level goes down, you feel the withdrawal symptoms. So, although some people smoke to wake themselves up, they end up being more tired.

Nicotine Addiction: The Facts

- ◉ When you smoke, your body becomes addicted to nicotine.

- ◉ It is very easy to become addicted to nicotine.

- ◉ Nicotine addiction makes you feel like you are stuck on a seesaw.

Nicotine Addiction

The main reason it is so difficult to quit smoking is that you become addicted to nicotine. In addition to nicotine addiction, several other factors make quitting a challenge. For one thing, smoking is a habit. Habits are hard to break. You may also feel that smoking helps keep your weight down or ease your stress. Any one of these reasons can make quitting difficult.

Let's look at why a few teens say they would have a difficult time giving up smoking.

Kate: Smoking Makes Me Thin

I was chubby when I started figure skating five years ago. I was the heaviest girl in my skating group. Right about that time, I started smoking with my friends and started to lose weight. I don't know if smoking helped me lose weight or not, but it seemed like a strange coincidence to me. Smoking always messes me up, though, because I have to stop skating to cough. My boyfriend is always complaining that I have bad breath, and I've also noticed that my teeth are looking kind of yellow. But I'm afraid to give up smoking because I have heard that people start to gain weight as soon as they quit. I can't be fat if I'm going to be a figure skater.

Kate believes that smoking keeps her thin, though she may have lost the weight because of the increased exercise of skating. Either way, she realizes that smoking causes problems with her lungs. Smoking makes it harder for her to have the strength to continue to skate. Kate should consider quitting smoking and starting a regular diet and exercise plan to supplement her skating regimen. She will feel better about herself knowing that she can maintain her proper body weight without smoking. Also, she will not suffer any of smoking's harmful side effects. An hour on the ice rink with her friends can give Kate an even better rush than puffing on a cigarette.

Vic: Smoking Kills My Shyness

I'm kind of quiet and shy around groups of people. Smoking helps ease my anxiety, especially when I am with a group of people I don't know very well. It gives me something to do with my hands. It also means that I won't be expected to talk a lot because I'm busy smoking.

Sometimes I'm the only one in the group who is smoking, and that makes me feel self-conscious, too. I just don't know what to do! Smoking helps me relax when I hang out with friends, but some people don't want to hang out with a smoker.

Vic uses smoking to lessen his shyness. Instead of facing his anxiety about meeting new people, Vic hides his fears behind cigarettes. He's actually hiding who he really is by using cigarettes. He is resisting the need to learn about himself. He isn't looking for the reason why he is so shy. If he figured that out, he wouldn't need smoking. He would also be able to control his anxiety when meeting new people. Vic needs to take steps to overcome his shyness instead of hiding behind cigarettes.

Nell: I Do It So Much, It Doesn't Seem Like a Big Deal

Believe it or not, when I light up a cigarette, most of the time I don't even realize that I've done it. Recently I almost got fired from a really good baby-sitting job because of my cigarette habit. One day the mother came home early, and I was holding the baby in one arm and a cigarette in the other hand. She was angry that I was smoking around her baby and exposing the baby to secondhand smoke. I promised never to do it again. Now I light up after I've finished baby-sitting. Sometimes it's really hard to go a couple of hours without smoking. I wish I had never started smoking.

Nell's story illustrates how smoking becomes an unconscious habit. Have you ever tried to break a habit? Perhaps you crack your knuckles, twirl your hair, or bite your fingernails. Someone might have pointed it out to you, and you didn't realize that you were even doing it. Try quitting one of your habits for just one day. You will probably find it to be harder than you thought.

Some people's smoking habits are linked directly to other habits. They might automatically light up a cigarette whenever they finish a meal, go to a party, or talk on the phone. When trying to kick the habit, it is important to identify when you smoke and to find something else to do with your hands and mouth during those times. You can chew gum or drink a cold glass of water instead of smoking during those times. If you feel fidgety, try to see how long your hands can remain in a still position. Each time, try to keep them still a little longer.

Bobby: Smoking Makes Me Calm

I started smoking when my parents were getting divorced. They used to yell at each other all the time, and that made me nervous. I started smoking to calm down. Cigarettes really got me through the tough times when things weren't going right for me. Now I smoke to stay calm and

Once someone is addicted to nicotine, it can seem like the only thing that helps relieve the stress of daily life is lighting a cigarette.

in control. The second I light up, I feel a sense of ease. I only feel jumpy when I can't get to a cig. Smoking gives me the boost I need to control all these things going on around me."

Bobby is experiencing the sadness and anxiety brought about by his parents' fighting and stress. He seeks comfort in cigarettes because he thinks that they ease the pain for him. However, Bobby should talk to someone about his problems, such as a teacher, counselor, friend, nurse, or doctor. These people can offer support and helpful advice better than a pack of cigarettes can, without being hazardous to Bobby's health.

Many people smoke to relieve the normal stress of everyday life. This isn't a good long-term solution. Long-term health problems such as lung cancer and heart problems aren't a good payoff for easing day-to-day stress. Nothing in your daily life is worth getting lung cancer or heart disease. Instead of smoking, try the following.

Calming Yourself Down

- ◎ Relax with a good book
- ◎ Take a nap
- ◎ Watch your favorite movie
- ◎ Soak in a bubble bath
- ◎ Have dinner or lunch with a good friend

Stomping Out Stress by Getting Energized

- ◎ Walk or jog
- ◎ Exercise or stretch
- ◎ Dance to your favorite music in your room
- ◎ Yell into your pillow to get it all out
- ◎ Work on your favorite hobby projects

If you anticipate a stressful situation coming up, such as a test or a big game, plan ahead. Take extra time for your healthy stress busters. Do not try to relieve your stress with something like smoking, which will only cause you harm.

Real Reasons Not to Smoke

- ◉ Smoking becomes a habit—A habit that causes bodily damage is a habit worth breaking!

- ◉ Smoking causes weight loss—There are many smokers who are overweight! Look around at the people who light up. Are they all skinny? Do they look very healthy? Exercise and a good diet will help you manage your weight and keep you healthy.

- ◉ It seems so natural, you forget about it—There are other things to do that are far more natural than turning your lungs black and making it hard to breathe. Just because it's easy to forget about doesn't mean that it isn't harming the body. It is.

- ◉ Smoking calms the nerves and relieves stress—While you may not be able to get rid of the things that cause stress in your life, you can change the way that you react to them. There are healthy ways to deal with stress, such as exercising and talking with friends. Smoking is not a healthy reaction to stress.

Chapter 4

Deciding Not to Smoke— Great Choice

You may have heard this expression before: "Kissing a smoker is like licking an ashtray." Smoker's breath has also been called zoo breath. And smelly breath isn't the only drag about a smoker. That cloud of smoke you see settles in the hair and clothes, too. Smoking also causes teeth to turn yellow or gray. It causes brown or yellow marks on the fingers as well.

Not smoking saves people around you. Secondhand smoke is the smoke that you see leaving a smoker's mouth. It is also the smoke that burns from a lit cigarette. There are more than four thousand chemicals, many of them harmful, in this smoke.

Some smokers make a point to blow it away from you or your friends. This doesn't stop the smoke from harming you. The health risks that the smoker faces are the same for someone who is breathing in the smoke. Secondhand smoke causes cancer. According to the ALA, it causes three thousand lung cancer deaths in the United States each year.

If your friends smoke, think about how it may be harming you. Many nonsmokers believe that smoking is disgusting. Some even think that it is a sign of weakness. If you're a smoker, you may be limiting the types of friends you can have. As a smoker, you'll be hanging out with other smokers or with people who don't care if your smoke is harming them.

Today it is nearly impossible to smoke in public places. Many state and local governments, as well as private companies, have imposed bans on smoking in places such as offices, restaurants, and stadiums. Public awareness about secondhand smoke and the dangers it poses for nonsmokers have made the bans acceptable and widespread.

If you still are not convinced, perhaps you have not looked at the price of cigarettes lately. In New York City, taxes in 2002 have increased the cost of one pack of cigarettes to $7.50. A pack-a-day habit will cost you $2,730 each year. Certainly you can think of better things to do with that money.

Smoking also limits your senses of taste and smell. Studies have shown that smoking gives you wrinkles and bad breath, and it makes your skin look unhealthy.

Seven Great Reasons Not to Smoke

- ◉ Smokers have stinky hair, breath, and clothes.

- ◉ Smoking can limit your social life. Nonsmokers do not want to be exposed to the health risks of smoking. Also, they do not like the stink of smoke. Nonsmokers may avoid smokers.

- ◉ Tough anti-smoking laws have made smoking illegal in public places such as offices, restaurants, and airplanes.

- ◉ Smoking limits your senses of taste and smell.

- ◉ Smoking gives you wrinkles and makes your skin look unhealthy.

- ◉ Smoking is expensive.

- ◉ Smoke and secondhand smoke cause certain kinds of cancer.

When Others Smoke

Let's say that you do not smoke. Think about riding in a car or being in a closed room with a smoker. The smoker's burning cigarette makes it hard for you to breathe. It may also drive you nuts because you know that the smoke is harming you. That is one of the reasons why antismoking laws exist across the country. These laws were designed to help and protect nonsmokers.

According to the ALA, a recent study done by the Environmental Protection Agency found that second-hand smoke causes at least three thousand lung cancer deaths each year in the United States. It also causes thirty-five thousand heart-related deaths each year. Secondhand smoke is also known as environmental tobacco smoke.

Understanding Secondhand Smoke

According to many organizations, there are two kinds of secondhand smoke:

- ◉ Mainstream smoke
- ◉ Sidestream smoke

Mainstream smoke is what the smoker inhales into his or her lungs and then releases into the air. Think of a smoker taking a drag in slow motion. The smoke passes through the filter of the cigarette. The filter traps some of the chemicals and tars. Then the smoke enters the lungs. The lungs filter out more of the harmful substances. Finally, the smoker exhales.

Sidestream smoke is the smoke that goes directly into the air from the tip of a burning cigarette. While this smoke may seem less harmless than mainstream, it actually isn't. According to the Canadian Lung Association, studies have shown that sidestream smoke contains many more chemicals than mainstream. Because it does not pass through a filter, it contains a lot more carbon monoxide, tars, and nicotine than mainstream smoke. The study also found that about 85 percent of secondhand smoke is sidestream smoke.

When a nonsmoker breathes in secondhand smoke, he or she breathes in the four thousand or so harmful chemicals of the smoke. Carbon monoxide can cause fatigue and headaches. The chemicals can also cause lung disease and heart disease. Studies have shown that nonsmokers who live with smokers die younger than people who live in smoke-free houses.

What does all this mean? The nonsmoker who lives or works with smokers can get sick from the smoke just as smokers can. Is that fair? What do you think?

Secondhand Smoke: The Risks

◎ The smoke from a cigarette can harm nonsmokers, too.

◎ Mainstream smoke is what a smoker inhales. It is filtered by the smoker's lungs. More poisonous to the nonsmoker is sidestream smoke, which contains all the unfiltered poisons— tars, carbon monoxide, and so on.

◎ The nonsmoker who lives or works with a smoker can also get sick from smoke.

Make Your Own Decision

Now you know more about smoking. You know how it affects your body, your appearance, and your health. You know more about why people start and why it is hard to stop.

Maybe you have not started smoking. Maybe your friends around you do, so you're considering it. Choosing whether to smoke is an important decision. The following test will help you. If you are already a smoker, try this test. It may change your mind about smoking.

This is the Smoker's Decision Test. It is not like a school test. There are no right or wrong answers. This is a way to help you get a clearer idea of what is important to you.

It will help you make a decision about smoking. Copy the columns onto a piece of notebook paper or make a photocopy of the test in order to mark your answers.

First, look closely at what you have checked in the Very Important column. Then proceed to part two.

Part One: Reasons for Smoking

	Very Important	Not Important
Smoking can make you feel like part of the group.	☐	☐
Smoking can make you feel more mature and glamorous.	☐	☐
If you already smoke, you would be giving up something that makes you feel good.	☐	☐
Smoking relaxes you.	☐	☐
You do not want to admit that it was a mistake to start smoking.	☐	☐
Quitting might cause you to gain weight.	☐	☐
You do not want to face the possibility that your smoking is out of control and you cannot quit.	☐	☐

Part Two: Reasons for Not Smoking

	Very Important	Not Important
Smoking can limit your social life.	☐	☐
Smoking is bad for your health. It can even kill you.	☐	☐
It is bad for the health of others around you.	☐	☐
Smoking has special health risks for women.	☐	☐
Most public places prohibit smoking.	☐	☐
It reduces athletic ability.	☐	☐
It is an expensive habit.	☐	☐
Smoking makes your breath, clothes, and hair smell bad.	☐	☐

Now write out your very important reasons for smoking and your very important reasons for not smoking. Compare them side by side.

Look at your reasons. Decide for yourself if you are going to start. If you have already started, decide if you are going to continue or quit. Either way, make your own decision.

Chapter 5

Quit Smoking Step by Step

If you are a smoker, you have probably tried to quit. You may have found that it is very hard. However, nearly half of all living adults who ever smoked have quit. That means there are millions of people who have quit smoking. You can, too. There is no guaranteed method; you have to find what is right for you. Here are some steps to follow to help you kick the habit.

List Your Reasons to Quit Smoking

Make a list of all the reasons that you want to quit. Your reasons don't have to be complicated.

- ◎ **To feel in control of your life**
- ◎ **To have better health**

- ◉ To save money

- ◉ To protect your family or friends from breathing secondhand smoke

- ◉ To feel free from addiction

Write down these reasons and keep the list with you every day. When you feel the urge to smoke, pull out the list and read it. Remind yourself: This is why I'm quitting.

Set a Date

Choose a special date to quit and mark it on the calendar. Do not change it. If you know that you smoke most often at school or work, choose a weekend to quit. That will make the first one or two days easier.

There are two ways to quit that have worked for others. One is to quit gradually. Smoke fewer and fewer cigarettes as you near your special date. This forces the body to adjust to lower and lower nicotine levels. Another way is to quit cold turkey. This means that you choose the special day to quit, and you smoke until that day and never again. People who quit cold turkey don't use excuses; they use willpower to stay in the "I am done smoking forever" frame of mind.

Cutting Down

Cutting down takes effort, but it is a good way to slowly adjust the body to the absence of nicotine. The trick to cutting down is monitoring your smoking habits. You probably smoke some cigarettes without even thinking about it. Other cigarettes, like the ones you smoke after a meal or a test, are more important to you. At those times you really want a cigarette. You need to decide which cigarette times are important to you and smoke only those cigarettes.

You can plan ahead of time. Carry the exact number of cigarettes you have decided to smoke that day. It might be just two or three. Another way to cut down is to smoke only half a cigarette at a time. You can also make cutting down easier by using a brand of cigarettes that you do not like. Icky-tasting cigarettes (ickier than your favorite) will help you not want to reach for them so much. Get rid of all your favorites and don't buy new ones.

Still another way is to delay having a cigarette when you want one. Instead of smoking when you want to, wait ten minutes. That way you can think it over and decide if you really want that cigarette. After ten minutes, you may not even want the cigarette anymore.

Change your smoking routine. Try keeping your cigarettes in a different place. Smoke with your other hand.

Don't do anything else when smoking and think about how you feel while you are doing it.

Cutting down is great, but do not fool yourself. You may think that you have things under control and that you can quit anytime. That is not true. Most people who cut down soon return to their original number of cigarettes.

Set your special quitting date!

Tell Everybody You Are Quitting

Tell your family and friends about your plan to quit smoking. That will make it harder for you to back out of it. It will also let others know that you might be cranky and a little hard to live with for a few days.

Do Not Change Your Eating Habits

Do not reach for a snack every time you want a cigarette. Chew gum. Exercise. If you snack on fatty foods or junk food, you might gain weight. People use weight gain as an excuse to start smoking again.

Reward Yourself

Find other things to do that are fun or make you happy. An easy choice is exercise. Exercise is good because you have to use your whole body. That reminds you of how important your lungs are. Also, exercise makes you feel good. Take up a hobby such as photography, music, or skateboarding. Go to the movies, the zoo, the beach, or a concert. To pay for these activities, use the money you are not spending on cigarettes!

Do Not Give Up—You Can Quit

If you smoke a cigarette or even an entire pack, do not feel that you have failed. Pull out your list and remind yourself why you want to quit. If your reasons have changed, make a new list. When you get the urge to smoke, do something else instead. Keep busy.

Watch for "smoke signals," like a friend lighting up. Know that this is the time when you are most likely to smoke. Be strong and do not give in to smoking. It will pay off.

Getting Help When You Want to Quit

You may believe that you cannot do it on your own. It's OK to need help. There are millions of people who have had to ask for help. Be proud of yourself for realizing your own limitations and understanding that you need help. Getting help is easy. Many organizations can help you overcome your smoking habit.

Check with your teacher, guidance counselor, or school nurse to find out if your school offers a program to help students kick the habit. If your school does not have such a program, ask your counselor to help you find a program. Perhaps you could channel the energy that comes from quitting smoking into starting a program at your school.

Three major organizations that are already in place and ready to help are the American Cancer Society, the American Lung Association, and the American Heart Association. All three have programs to help you stop smoking. For information on contacting these organizations, look in the Where to Go for Help section of this book.

Help can come from several sources. Your doctor can prescribe medicine to help break the addiction. Some people succeed in quitting smoking by using special chewing gum. Others find help by using a nicotine patch, which is a small pad (similar to a bandage) that, when placed on your body, releases small amounts of nicotine into your skin. It gives your body the nicotine it craves without all the other harmful chemicals in a cigarette. Both the gum and the patch can help steer your body away from nicotine.

You may find it helpful to get some counseling. Deciding to quit smoking is a major step and can create feelings of stress, unhappiness, and irritability. You may have to cope with changing emotions in addition to coping with fighting your nicotine cravings.

Sometimes it helps to have someone to talk to, who will listen to you and offer you the support you need to get through this.

Now you know much more about smoking. Do you still find smoking hip and glamorous? You have learned about the health risks associated with smoking as well as how smoking affects your social life. If you are still curious about smoking, get all the facts before you take that first puff from a cigarette, cigar, or pipe. Smoking is a dead end—literally—so deciding to smoke is not a casual choice. Make this important decision while respecting yourself. You are important and you deserve good health. If you are already addicted and you want to quit smoking, remember that there are people and organizations that can help you on the road to recovery. You've made a great choice for better health, and you deserve to get smoking and nicotine out of your life.

Glossary

addictive Causing a person's body to depend on a chemical.

adrenal gland A gland that produces the hormone adrenaline. Adrenaline prepares the body for emergency action; it makes the heart work harder.

bronchi Tubes in the lungs.

bronchitis A condition marked by severe coughing and irritation of the lungs that is often caused by smoking.

cancer A disease that causes cells to grow abnormally and become tumors. These tumors spread and interfere with normal cell growth.

carbon dioxide A gas that is breathed out of the body during exhalation.

carbon monoxide A gas that is poisonous. It is one of the chemicals in cigarette smoke.

cilia Tiny hairs in the bronchi that clear away mucus.

craving A great desire or longing.

drag The inhalation of cigarette smoke.

emphysema A severe lung disease.

glamorous Full of excitement and romance.

heart disease One of a number of health problems such as heart attack, stroke, hardening of the arteries, and blood clots.

influence To sway or affect.

lung cancer A disease in which the cells of the lungs divide uncontrollably. Smoking is a major cause of lung cancer.

mainstream smoke What the smoker inhales and exhales.

mucus A slippery secretion that coats and protects mucous membranes.

nicotine A drug found in tobacco to which your body becomes addicted.

premature Early; before being fully ready.

sidestream smoke The smoke that comes from the burning end of a cigarette.

stress Tension or pressure.

tar A sticky black substance found in tobacco. It coats the lungs when smoke is inhaled.

withdrawal The process of stopping the body's dependency on an addictive drug; physical and mental effects an addict suffers after ceasing to take an addictive drug.

Where to Go for Help

Organizations

American Cancer Society (ACS)
National Home Office
1599 Clifton Road
Atlanta, GA 30329
(800) ACS-2345 (227-2345)
Web site: http://www.cancer.org

American Lung Association (ALA)
61 Broadway, Sixth Floor
New York, NY 10006
(800) LUNG-USA (586-4872)
(212) 315-8700
Web site: http://www.lungusa.org

Office on Smoking and Health (OSH), Centers for
    Disease Control and Prevention (CDC)
4770 Buford Highway NE, Mail Stop K50
Atlanta, GA 30341-3724
(800) CDC-1311 (232-1311)
(770) 488-5705
Web site: http://www.cdc.gov/tobacco

In Canada

Canadian Cancer Society
10 Alcorn Avenue, Suite 200
Toronto, ON M4V 3B1
(888) 939-3333
(416) 961-7223
Web site: http://www.cancer.ca

Canadian Lung Association National Office
3 Raymond Street, Suite 300
Ottawa, ON K1R 1A3
(888) 566-LUNG (566-5864)
(613) 569-6411
Web site: http://www.lung.ca

National Clearinghouse on Tobacco and Health,
    Canadian Council for Tobacco Control (CCTC)
75 Albert Street, Suite 508
Ottawa, ON K1P 5E7

(800) 267-5234
(613) 567-3050
Web site: http://www.ncth.ca/NCTHweb.nsf

Web Sites

Due to the changing nature of Internet links, the Rosen
Publishing Group, Inc., has developed an online list of
Web sites related to the subject of this book. This site is
updated regularly. Please use this link to access the list:

http://www.rosenlinks.com/ntk/smok

For Further Reading

DeAngelis, Gina. *Nicotine and Cigarettes*. New York: Chelsea House, 1999.

Fisher, Edwin B., Jr., Ph.D., and Toni L. Goldfarb. *American Lung Association: 7 Steps to a Smoke-Free Life*. New York: John Wiley and Sons, 1998.

Gebhardt, Jack. *Help Your Smoker Quit: A Radically Happy Strategy for Nonsmoking Parents, Kids, Spouses, and Friends*. Minneapolis: Fairview Press, 1998.

Heyes, Eileen. *Tobacco USA: The Industry Behind the Smoke Curtain*. Brookfield, CT: Millbrook Press, 1999.

Moe, Barbara A. *Teen Smoking and Tobacco Use*. Springfield, NJ: Enslow Publishers, 2000.

Morgan, Sally. *Smoking*. New York: Raintree Publishers, 2002.

Torr, James D. *Smoking*. San Diego: Greenhaven Press, 2001.

Bibliography

American Lung Association. "American Lung Association Fact Sheet: Teenage Tobacco Use." June 2002. Retrieved October 1, 2002 (http://www.lungusa.org/tobacco/teenager_factsheet99.html).

American Lung Association. "American Lung Association Fact Sheet: Tobacco-Free Schools." 2002. Retrieved October 1, 2002 (http://www.lungusa.org/tobacco/schools_factsheet99.html).

Centers for Disease Control and Prevention. "Tobacco Use in the United States." 1999–2001. Retrieved October 1, 2002 (http://www.cdc.gov/tobacco/overview/tobus_us.htm).

Centers for Disease Control and Prevention. "You Can Quit Smoking Consumer Guide." Retrieved October 1, 2002 (http://www.cdc.gov/tobacco/quit/canquit.htm).

Index

About the Author

Elizabeth Keyishian is an associate editor for an award-winning children's science magazine. In addition to writing for young adults, she has published humorous essays. A graduate of Wesleyan University, Ms. Keyishian lives in New York City.

About the Series Editor

Evan Stark is a well-known sociologist, educator, and therapist as well as a popular lecturer on women's and children's health issues. Dr. Stark was a Henry Rutgers Fellow at Rutgers University, an associate at the Institution for Social and Policy Studies at Yale University, and a Fulbright Fellow at the University of Essex. He is the author of many publications in the field of family relations and is the father of four children.

Photo Credits

Series Designer: Tom Forget